theol

Cynthia Bourgeault

The Corner of
Fourth and Nondual

Fortress Press

Minneapolis

THE CORNER OF FOURTH AND NONDUAL

Originally published by Darton, Longman,
and Todd London, UK
Copyright © 2022 Cynthia Bourgeault. Published by
Fortress Press, an imprint of 1517 Media.

Print ISBN: 978-1-5064-8449-5
eBook ISBN: 978-1-5064-8450-1

Cover design: Kristin Miller

Contents

1

The iCloud of Unknowing

THE FIRST AND most distinguishing character-
istic of my work is that it's *practice-based*. By
this I mean that everything I think, know, or
write about emerges out of a daily rule of life
grounded in the classic Benedictine rhythm of
ora et labora, 'prayer and work,' anchored by
two daily periods of sitting meditation, morn-
ing and evening.

This may not strike you as anything
particularly remarkable. I am still probably
most widely known a teacher of Centering
Prayer, and when you're in the Centering Prayer
movement, that's just what you do. But in fact,
the foundations of this spiritual habit were laid
decades before I'd ever even heard of Centering
Prayer and actually have less to do with personal
devotion than with the hermeneutics of seeing.
Centering Prayer is my 'go to' practice to keep
the lens of perception clear.

I learned the difference between thinking and knowing very young in life through the fortuitous but at the time distinctly uncomfortable circumstances of my early upbringing when I found myself being shoved down two diametrically opposing pathways of spiritual knowledge at the same time. My mother was a faithful Christian Scientist, and from the time I was a toddler until my eighteenth birthday I was a dutiful conscript at Christian Science Sunday School, where we memorized long metaphysical formulas demonstrating the triumph of 'infinite mind' over 'mortal error'. But my mother was also a strong a believer in Quaker education, and somehow funds were scraped together to send me to the local Quaker school for the early years of my education. Meeting for Worship was an unvarying part of the weekly curriculum, and in our corner of southeastern Pennsylvania, the cradle of American Quakerism, that meant *silent* meeting for worship.

Schoolbooks closed early on Thursday

afternoons as the dismissal bell rang a little before two o'clock to announce meeting for worship. The entire student body, ages five to twelve, trooped into the cavernous old meeting house, and we took our seats on simple benches, well-worn from already two centuries of continuous use. I remember gazing up at the light filtering through the clerestory window and feeling a quiet spaciousness opening up inside me. After a while, the fidgeting and restlessness would settle down and the whole room would gradually fall into a sweet and intimate silence, punctuated occasionally by someone rising to offer a small bit of scripture or a prayer. In that enfolding silence, surrounded by the presence of Quakers who'd gone before, I experienced my first taste of what you might call 'wordless presence'. And I knew I could trust it.

Fast forward thirty years, to 1989. I am by now an Episcopal priest, with ten years of service under my belt. I have a PhD in Medieval Literature, earned nearly a decade earlier and never put to full use, though I have done a fair bit of scholarly writing on the fourteenth-century spiritual classic *The Cloud of Unknowing*. I have at this point worked in a variety of parishes from Philadelphia to coastal Maine, chiefly in a teaching capacity. My parishioners are by and large well educated, verbal, and contentious. They like to argue about the creeds. I enjoy the intellectual jousts but escape whenever I can to the Benedictine monastic watering holes that have increasingly become my spiritual lifelines. I am vaguely aware that something is missing.

Little did I know that the missing piece would fall dramatically into place a few months later when I signed up on a whim for a week-long Centering Prayer Intensive retreat at St Benedict's Monastery in Snowmass, Colorado. It was not ten minutes into my first sit before I found myself back in the rambling old Friends meeting house, back in that same indescribable sense of intimacy and presence. I knew I was finally home.

Centering Prayer

Let me say just a few words here about the method of Centering Prayer since it's actually an important part of the story. This simple, no-frills meditation method was developed in the 1970s by Fr Thomas Keating and a small group of his fellow Benedictine Trappists to offer a Christian alternative to the Eastern meditation methods, which at the time were making major inroads in the West. Like most meditation methods it aims to break the cycle of compulsive, associative thinking that usurps most of our waking consciousness. But it does this this in a somewhat nontraditional way. Unlike most beginning meditation practices, which provide a simple object of focus for the attention (like following the breath or reciting a mantra), Centering Prayer provides no such focal point; it merely teaches the practitioner how to release the attention promptly when it gets tangled up in a thought. Echoing the teaching of *The Cloud of Unknowing* (which turned out to be Centering Prayer's principal source), a 'thought' is defined as anything that brings attention to a focal point – 'as the eye of an archer is upon the target he is shooting at', the anonymous medieval author illustrates. His instruction is to immediately release the object of attention and return to the 'cloud of unknowing', his metaphor for a more diffuse, objectless awareness which he sees as the foundational prerequisite for what he calls 'the work of contemplation'. Centering Prayer provides a simple method for doing just that. For twenty minutes the practitioner sits, eyes closed, in a state of gentle receptivity. When thoughts intrude, one simply 'lets them go', typically utilizing a short, self-chosen 'sacred word' as a mnemonic device to help facilitate this prompt release – again based on counsel from *The Cloud of Unknowing*.

It was of course more than a little serendipitous to me to see my two worlds coming back together again, as a scholar of *The Cloud of Unknowing* and now as a would-be practitioner along its path. When I returned to my parish in Maine, I of course started a Centering Prayer group, and it took off immediately. People were clearly excited to discover this contemplative treasure in their own Christian backyard. The most gratifying part of it for me, however, was that I began to notice that the people in my community who really took on Centering Prayer were slowly but incrementally beginning to think differently. I don't mean simply what they thought, but *how* they thought. Their theology was becoming less propositional, far less argumentative. Listening deepened. Issues diminished in importance. Inclusive language stopped being the deal-breaker. There seemed to be a growing willingness to simply stand together in that 'cloud of unknowing' and let the Mystery reveal itself. Through Centering Prayer, we were all learning to let go of that downed electric wire of habitual subject/object-polarized thinking and make room for each other, and for God.

And the day came when we were finally

ready to tackle *The Cloud of Unknowing* head on.

I had forestalled this encounter for as long as I could, believe it or not. You might have thought that it would be an obvious starting point, given my academic background here, but because I knew the Cloud so well, I also knew what pitfalls lay in store. If truth be told, I was still licking my wounds from a first disastrous attempt in this regard a dozen years earlier at a university parish I was then serving. We got as far as Chapter 3 before I found myself hard up against those notoriously challenging opening instructions:

> Lift up your heart unto God with a meek stirring of love, and intend by that himself and none of his goods. And to that end, be loath to think on anything but on himself so that nothing works in your mind or in your will but only himself. And to do that in yourself is to forget all the creatures that ever God made and their works so that your thoughts and your desires are not directed or stretched to any of them, either

16

in general or in specific. But let them be, and take no notice of them.[1]

My theologically sophisticated parishioners were having none of it. 'Forget all the creatures that ever God made?' 'But aren't we supposed to *love* the world? Didn't God so love the world that he sent his only son?' 'But what about "and God saw that it was good"?' '... sounds like more of the same world-hating, soul-denying asceticism ...' 'sounds like spiritual bypassing ...' 'But what about the poor and marginalized? Aren't we supposed to take notice of *them*?' In less than ten minutes *The Cloud of Unknowing* was weighed in the balance and found wanting. Never again, I vowed.

This time it was different, however. To my surprise, my Centering Prayer-trained students were actually getting it, and with relative ease. Those months of sitting on the cushion had taught them to see something different – or different*ly*, perhaps; they could

[1] *The Cloud of Unknowing*, Chapter 5-2 (translation from the Middle English my own).

17

begin to crack the code. They knew now that 'creature' didn't mean a furry animal created by God; it meant the *object of their attention*. It meant a *thought,* and the instruction in Centering Prayer is 'just let them go'. They had learned from practice that grabbing onto a thought simply pulls you back into the orbit of rational thinking; real contemplation lies beyond. They were beginning to grasp subtle cues that are missed when the rational mind attempts to wrap its tentacles around trans-rational phenomena. Above all, they recognized the genre they were dealing with: not a theological treatise on Christian love, but a highly sophisticated spiritual manual written in technical and perhaps even coded language, toward the attainment of a higher state of consciousness.

The Cloud of Unknowing is usually classified by scholars as one of the high exemplars of late-monastic love mysticism. Over the years of working with this text, I have come to believe that it is actually the earliest treatise on the phenomenology of consciousness in the Christian West, framed in categories strikingly compatible with the insights of Tibetan Buddhism and contemporary neurobiology. This unknown medieval author is already onto the symbiotic feedback loop between the 'objectification' of attention and the illusion of a phenomenal selfhood or 'I'. And he senses with precocious clarity that what the West calls contemplation and what the East calls 'nondual realization' has everything to do *with the stabilization of consciousness beyond the subject/object split.* Once you penetrate his metaphors and allow yourself to see what he is actually saying here, it takes your breath away.

But I would never even have remotely discovered this had it not been for my own steady, incremental practice of Centering Prayer. I never had a clue about it all those years I was working with this text as a scholar. It was only after repeated confirmation on the prayer mat that grabbing onto a thought, no matter how seductive, would inevitably result in throwing me back into a more constricted field of awareness and the familiar mental rut tracks, that I learned to prefer, and ultimately even navigate a bit, within the 'cloud' of objectiveless awareness. Until this knowledge was ground-truthed in me, there was no way I could even recognize the lifeline this text was offering me.

That is how I gradually came to learn that that when you are working with mystical texts, there is a direct feedback loop between the text and your own inner contemplative ground. The two leverage each other, gradually extending the radius of seeing. This is in fact time-honored hermetic principle: 'Like knows like.' To understand a mystical text, you have to begin by entraining with it, entering it through the cave of your own heart.

I am not using the word 'heart' metaphorically here. Throughout the Western Inner tradition, the heart is widely regarded as the primary instrument of divine insight, a principle first articulated by Jesus himself: 'Blessed are the pure in heart, for they shall see God.' When the heart is purified (i.e. freed of its captivity to the rational mind and personal emotional drama), it can assume its true function as *an organ of spiritual perception*, directly aligning itself with a greater clairvoyance that is in fact objective because it corresponds to an order of reality far higher and more coherent than the dichotomized mental projections we mistake for 'objective' in our own upside-down world. I have come to think of this, only half-jokingly, as the 'icloud of unknowing', from which mystical truth, seamless and whole, can be holographically downloaded by every attuned human heart, no matter how widely separated in physical time and space.

I realize that this may sound like malarkey to those whose hermeneutical methods are entirely staked upon the rational mind. How can one establish 'standards' to demonstrate that the knowledge obtained through contemplative insight – jagged, seamless, surprising, coming out of left field, requiring a quantum mental leap to follow, and resting on an invincible inner authority – is anything other than narcissistic madness? How can I 'prove' that there is such a thing as higher objective knowledge and that it has its own rigorous methods for external validation and its own ways of eventually weeding the sheep from the goats?

But I guess I've staked my life on the truth of this wager. My initial childhood learning, delivered in the cognitive dissonance between that elaborate mental construction I recognized as 'false' and the gentle inner knowingness I recognized as 'true' became the fundamental divining rod for my life journey. There would be much to learn, painful purifications in store as I slowly discovered what those methods of external validation were and what they entailed. But the more than compensating joy in all this has been a slow penetration into a deeper understanding of what contemplation meant, originally, to those great patristic divines who first used the term: not 'resting in God,' as we tend to think of it nowadays, but *luminous seeing*. 'Knowledge impregnated by love' as the sixth-century teacher John Chrysostom described it, and as the author of *The Cloud of Unknowing* rediscovered in his own way. Not the emotion of love, but a quiet, clairvoyant intimacy, physically grounded in the human heart.

I share this with you now for one other reason, which is that most of the theologians I have been most deeply drawn to over the decades and who have most deeply impacted my own work all tend to think in this way. You will meet some of them in the course of this work: Jacob Boehme, Teilhard de Chardin, Beatrice Bruteau, Bruno Barnhart, Thomas Keating – not to mention, of course, Jesus himself. They are all what I'd call 'cosmogonic mystics'. They peer straight into the heart of things, ask the unaskable questions (like 'why did anything come into being in the first place?') and find their answers through a direct inner seeing which they then proceed to unpack with an astounding inner authority and coherence, let the chips fall where they may. These are the people who have deeply watered my soul, and in learning to see *what*

23

they see, I have also had to learn *how* they see, for this is the only way the access route actually opens up. This comes with no special claims to spiritual giftedness. But to the extent that the underlying hermeneutical wager is true – that the quietened and energetically collected heart actually participates holographically in a more universal and objective knowingness – the time logged on the meditation cushion confers its immediate payback in the enhanced ability to enter into spiritual entrainment with these extraordinary spiritual seers whose insights, I believe, hold the key to disentangling from some of the theological cul de sacs in which the pure genius of the Christian transformative vision has too long been held captive.

So I practise daily: the psalms, the Centering Prayer, welcoming the divine immediacy when it comes. I try to live my day in some sort of conscious dialogue with the Benedictine Rule as an ordering rhythm. As the Quaker Isaac Penington put it: 'There is a great difference between comprehending the knowledge of things and tasting the hidden life of them.' I have tried as much as possible to do my theology on the 'tasting' side of the equation.

2
Theodyssey

FUNDAMENTALLY, MY THEOLOGY is pretty orthodox. It travels in an elliptical arc between those two great cornerstones of Christian theological seeing, the incarnation and the Paschal Mystery. Jesus is a real presence to me, not simply a 'Christ consciousness', and the eucharist is the epicenter of this presence. The Trinity is the tie-rod, connecting the created and uncreated worlds in a single unified field of creative exchange.

What makes my theology initially exotic, however, is that I don't derive the foundational truths of the Christian path from the usual Biblical and theological starting points. My cosmology is not the biblical flat earth, but the fourteen-billion-year-old universe story science now lays before us, extended yet more broadly yet to incorporate the invisible realms depicted in the traditional *sophia perennis* cosmology as 'the great chain of being'. And the centrality of the paschal mystery does not rest on classic atonement theology, but on the Christian cosmogonic mysticism of visionaries like Jacob Boehme and Teilhard de Chardin that set the Christ mystery within its broadest and deepest cosmogonic scope.

'Unless [Christianity] is understood to be the most realistic and cosmic of faiths and hopes, nothing has been understood of its "mysteries",' writes Pierre Teilhard de Chardin in the final pages of his masterwork, *The Human Phenomenon*.[2] By 'realistic' he means capable of validation within the real world, not simply as theological glass bead game or an interior landscape of myth and metaphor. By 'cosmic' he means coextensive with the actual dimensions of the created order and still fully intelligible and coherent at that scale. That is my assessment as well, and it has set the basic agenda for my theology.

[2] Sarah Appleton-Weber, ed., *The Human Phenomenon: Pierre Teilhard de Chardin* (Eastbourne, Brighton, and Chicago: Sussex Academic Press, 1999), p. 211.

At a time when significant numbers of my generation were giving up on Christianity as irrelevant, unintelligible, or desperately in need of pruning, my sense was always the opposite: that Christianity had simply become potbound, like the teetering jade plant that once sat on my windowsill: trapped in a cosmology and theological superstructure by now far too small to contain the vast life force that still ran through its veins. The solution, it seemed to me, lay not in the direction of pruning – demythologizing, rationalizing, secularizing, downsizing the scale of the mystery – but rather, in the direction of repotting this poor plant in a larger container, with more fertile soil, where it might have room to grow.

In this work my two primary partners have been Jacob Boehme and Teilhard de Chardin, both of them cosmogonic mystics who radically pushed the envelope of Christian cosmological imagination while remaining unswervingly anchored in an absolutely Christocentric bedrock. Teilhard, a paleontologist by training, was the first to transpose the Christian metanarrative to the dimensions of today's known universe: fourteen billion years in duration, fathomless in expanse. For him the long arc of history was measured in geological eons, not historical generations, and he urged his readers to open their eyes and truly see – *feel* – the scale of the thing: 'the sense of spatial immensity ... the sense of depth ... the sense of number ... the sense of movement, capable of perceiving the irresistible developments hidden in the immensely slow ....'[3] Do not be afraid, he reassures us: at this scale the Christian Mystery not only holds its own but at last comes into its own. In a remarkable spiritual *tour de force* he unfolds a sweeping vision of salvation history, stretching across the geological ages from its headwaters in 'the unorganized multitude' to its final implosion at the Omega Point, when all that was originally sewn into the cosmos as evolutionary seed is harvested as realized Love. In this cosmic journey Christ emerges – at first implicitly, then

[3]   Ibid., p. 5.

fully revealed – as the one holding the reins of evolution, guiding the entire unfolding from its inchoate beginnings to its triumphant end. 'Cosmogenesis has become Christogenesis' is the Teilhardian meme par excellence.

If Teilhard's eye is on the Omega Point, Boehme's is on the alpha point. How did anything come into being in the first place, he wondered – or in his own words, 'How did the endless unity bring itself into something somethingness?' It's a question I daresay few of us have ever seriously dwelled on. The conventional theological accounts assume that the 'reason' for creation is because 'God is love'. The visible world came into being out of an effulgence of divine goodness, for our benefit and joy, because that's what love does. This certainly meets the conventional requirements, but for a more quizzical frame of mind, the hard question still remains: what is it about love that requires it to project itself outwardly to fulfill itself – or as the case may be, relieve itself? Why does it not simply remain locked up within the endless unity?

This may seem at first like an impertinent speculation – a prying into the inner fastnesses of God. But it is this question, and this question alone, I believe, that provides the only really satisfying answer to the question of why Jesus is in fact the cosmic redeemer of the world. Nothing else reaches deep enough, once Adam and Eve have dropped out of the equation and you are hard up against the question, 'What is being atoned for? And why?' Atonement is incontrovertibly real, and all attempts to sidestep it or downsize it wind up in a bloodless Christianity and a cheapened and desacralized universe. But the roots of this mystery go back way further than simply human misdoing. They lie deep within the hidden abyss of God.

Jacob Boehme was not afraid to go there. An unlettered shoemaker by trade, living an outwardly conventional life in a small German village, he would hardly be seen as a prime candidate for storming the gates of heaven. But on the inside he was racked by the fire of his searching heart, and one fateful day in the year 1600 the gates of heaven stormed *him*. As he sat idly gazing at a pewter dish sparkling in the sunlight, he suddenly found himself swept up in such a firestorm of unitive seeing that 'in one quarter of an hour I saw and I knew more than if I had been many years together at a university.'[4] He spent the rest of his relatively brief life trying to unpack what he had received in that brief, timeless moment.

What emerged out of that seeing was perhaps the most intricate and brilliant cosmogony I have ever encountered. In a way I have seen nowhere else he was able to demonstrate why the proverbial 'crack that runs through everything' – manifesting in our own earth realm in the all too real reality of sin and fallenness – has its origin in the original cracking of the divine heart ('into divisibility and perceptivity,' Boehme would say) which is the costly and altogether necessary price of anything arising at all. It is the price borne equally between infinitude and finitude for the

[4] Jacob Boehme, *The Confessions of Jacob Boehme*, ed. Evelyn Underhill (Whitefish, MT: Kessinger, n.d.), p. 41.

alchemical creation of love out of the fires of yearning and desire. Boehme makes his case brilliantly without falling even for an instant into an ontological dualism (good God, evil God), by folding it into a sevenfold cosmogonic process in which *wrath* (fire, darkness, anguish) furnishes the necessary matrix for the emergence of light, and out of light, *agape love*.

This same sevenfold process, written in our own hearts, becomes our pathway to transfiguration if we walk it humbly but fearlessly, in the presence of Christ who is – *must* – be there to help carry the burden which is not ours alone to bear. Both sacramentally and through his intimate presence he is the guardian of our safe passage as we risk the crucifixion of our wills for the resurrection of our hearts.

In a breathtaking weaving, Boehme brings together cosmology, sacrament, and personal piety to create a Christian cosmovision which is both internally consistent and numinously compelling. It is a staggering achievement, really, and I bring it forward here not as a thumbnail exegesis of Boehme, but as a window into my own theology. What speaks to me most deeply in both Boehme and Teilhard is 'the achieve of, the mastery of it': the wingspan of their windhover hearts calling forth the wingspan of my own. Perhaps it was those long years of cognitive dissonance when I was caught in the crossfire between my Christian Science head and my Quaker heart, but I have never lost faith that there *is* such a thing as a unified Christian cosmovision that is vast enough to span the eons and tender enough to hold Jesus Christ at its epicenter. And my own theology, for better or worse, has been a life's journey – a 'theodyssey' if you want to call it that – to live that wager into reality.

In that spirit, then, I would like to attempt to lay before you now the cosmogonic premises on which my theology is built. You'll see the hands of Boehme and Teilhard at work here, but the synthesis is finally my own.

- This physical earth is neither illusory nor unreal. It is dense, yes, ploddingly binary and ponderous in this way. It moves always stepwise. The seeing heart can outrun it instantly. But this density is not a punishment for fallenness, but rather, the exact and *only* condition in which the holiest of the holy of all miracles can unfold: the full revelation of the divine heart.

- The reasons for both creation and redemption are more complex than classical theology acknowledges and ultimately reside not in human fallenness but in the same innermost mystery of the divine heart. 'I was a hidden treasure and I loved to be known, and so I created the worlds seen and unseen,' in the words of a well-loved Islamic mystical saying – a statement with which Jacob Boehme would not disagree. The primordial yearning – in whose image and likeness we are made – is the yearning to be seen; to reveal ourself fully to another and be received in love. It is like that for God as well; that is the root of the root of all manifestation.

- Love is not the alpha of creation, but the omega. It is not the starting point of the journey, but its final destination. The created order did not come into an existence as the effulgence of a divine love already fully realized in itself, but rather as the vast and intricate vehicle of its full realization. *Agape* love does not exist in a 'natural' state. It is an alchemical substance, forged when the raw primal force, *eros*, is subjected to the sacramental act of surrender, *or kenosis*. My formula for this is $a=ek$. It is the reason why finitude is a necessary condition for the final revelation of love; it furnishes the backboard for surrender. Without it, eros, untransformed, would simply go on grasping and generating and attracting for all eternity. When constricted by finitude, it finally bears fruit.

- Because the conditions here are hard, 'God sent his only son.' To accompany us, to shield us and to gentle our path so that we do not despair. The conditions must remain as they are, but we do not bear them alone, and Jesus' willing kenosis on the cross furnishes both the model and the sacramental foretaste of the transfigured love that awaits us in full as we too become capable of such depths of self-offering. All things in the created order begin in fire and end in light, teaches Boehme, and as we are willing to entrust our lives to the alchemical fire, pain is not an opposing force, but 'the ground of motion: 'the first step in a journey whose ultimate fulfillment is the redemption of all things in love.

• Suffering is real, ontologically necessary, and sacramental. I am not talking here about *stupid suffering*, our own conscious or unconscious complicity in stoking the fire. But beyond that, there remains an irreducible suffering which is the cost of manifestation itself, and the more we become clear and mature in our own being, the more we are both able and willing to take a part of that on. As we do this, our own lives become part of the continuing alchemy of divine love.

- The Trinity is the cosmogonic principle through which everything comes into existence.

- Unitive or nondual oneness does not cancel out, melt, or override particularity, but rather *transfigures* it – in a 'paroxysm of harmonized complexity,' to quote Teilhard de Chardin[5] – like sunlight shining through a stained-glass window which draws the whole complex assemblage into a single radiance. In a Western and Christian vision of unitive attainment, both the One and the particular are to be preserved, for these are the conditions through which love – the ultimate unity – is made manifest.

[5] Teilhard, p.186.

MY THEOLOGY — CYNTHIA BOURGEAULT

This is my theology in a nutshell – or perhaps, more accurately, in a flowerpot. While this new flowerpot may take a bit of getting used to, my eyes remain on the jade, to see if it will grow.

3

'Two's Company, Three's a World …'

I SHOULD PROBABLY share a bit more here about my take on the Trinity, for it is certainly one of the more unusual features of my theology. I can be clearly situated within a growing circle of contemporary theologians (including Raimon Panikkar, Catherine Lacugna, Beatrice Bruteau, and Richard Rohr) who have brought a renewed emphasis to the Trinity as a cornerstone of Christian identity. But I push beyond any of these others in envisioning the Trinity as a *cosmogonic principle*, the fundamental generative mechanism through which all things came into being.

Beatrice Bruteau admittedly comes close in her brilliant 1997 book *God's Ecstasy: The Creation of a Self-Creating World*. Bruteau, whom I am honoured to claim as one of my personal mentors, was a mathematician as well as a theologian, with advanced degrees in both disciplines. In *God's Ecstasy* she takes a close look at the principle of symbiotic unity, acknowledged by scientists as a fundamental evolutionary driveshaft. 'Symbiotic unity' means differentiation of function within an overall structural unity. You see it quintessentially in a cell, where individual components perform different but complementary functions, creating a whole that is greater than the sum of its parts. Fundamentally, however the process gets underway far earlier than the cell: two hydrogen molecules come together with one oxygen, and a whole new substance – water – appears. And you can push things back even further, back to the atoms and subatomic particles; it's symbiotic unity all the way down. Exactly the same symbiotic unity Bruteau saw reflected in the 'three God persons in community', as she described the Trinity: three in one, unique in function but one in Godhood, circumscribing a relational field of 'agape love' that is inherently creative and self-projective. 'It is the presence of the Trinity as a pattern repeated at every scale of the cosmic order,' she feels, 'that makes the universe the manifestation of God and itself sacred and holy'.[6]

Now I may be a curmudgeon here, but I have always resisted a kind of approach that too easily conflates theology with cosmogonics. Bruteau's argument rests on the premise that there are, in fact, three primordial 'God persons in community', a stipulation pretty much limited to the Christian faith community. Her argument is elegant when received within an exclusively Christian faith-generated cosmology, but would hold little currency for a Muslim, a Hindu, or a Buddhist, and for me, this is a fatal weak link. You simply can't derive a universal law assumed to be binding 'at every scale of the cosmic order' from an *a priori* and highly site-specific theological assumption. Objective truth has to go deeper.

I believe that there *is* in fact, a primordial relational field out there, and that its energetic signature is ultimately, as Bruteau claims,

[6] Beatrice Bruteau, *God's Ecstasy: The Creation of a Self-Creating World* (New York: Crossroad, 1997), p. 14.

47

'agape love'. But the three God-persons in community are not ultimately the cause of it. They are in fact *exemplars* – personifications – of an even more fundamental cosmogonic principle which governs how 'somethingness emerges out of nothing' in the first place.

The name of this more primordial law is 'The Law of Three'. And I first was introduced to it through my now-thirty-five-year immersion in the Gurdjieff Work.

The Gurdjieff Perspective

The *what*? I can just see the eyes rolling just now. Am I really proposing to offer serious theological standing to an obscure esoteric principle promulgated by an early-twentieth-century Russian-Armenian spiritual teacher still widely regarded as a charlatan? But yes, that's indeed where I'm headed. Partly because the Gurdjieff teaching as a whole has been seriously underestimated, especially in its inherent affinity with core Christian reference points. But more because I believe that the Law of Three is indeed an empirically verifiable principle that turns out to have far more universal intelligibility, not to mention cosmogonic clout, than a presumed 'three God persons in community'.

The name G. I. Gurdjieff first appeared on my radar screen back in 1982 by way of a casual mention in Jacob Needleman's iconic book *Lost Christianity*. The book galvanized me; it seemed to be speaking directly to the unanswered questions of my own heart, and I soon found my way to the Gurdjieff teaching itself and not long afterwards into 'the Work', the name familiarly given to the formal network of groups, spread across several continents, that devote themselves to the practical study of this teaching. We got off to a bit of a rocky start, partly because my clergy collar was regarded with suspicion in some quarters, but more because I was still back in those days a quintessential talking head, filled with ideas and theories, and prone to holding forth. As I would slowly learn, this Work was about something else, some other quality of attention which in the long run would prove to be much more helpful. Gradually we all settled in with each other, and it was under the patient tutelage of some of the more remarkable human beings I have ever met on this planet that the Law of Three jumped off the pages of the book to become a living reality for me.

The Law of Three is also known in the Work as 'the Law of World Creation'. It basically stipulates that every phenomenon, at whatever scale (from the subatomic to the cosmic) and in whatever domain (scientific, sociological, political, literary, personal) arises from the interaction of three independent forces, or lines of action. These are variously known as 'affirming', 'denying', and 'reconciling', or sometimes simply as 'first', 'second', and 'third'. *Affirming* is the pushing force, the energy driving the process forward. *Denying* is the push-back, which can present itself either as active resistance or simply as the medium through which an action flows. *Reconciling* breaks the impasse between these two forces and allows them to come into a creative interweaving: a new synthesis, with its own integrity and creative potential.

'But that's just Hegel!' you say: thesis, antithesis, synthesis. But look more closely. In the Hegelian scenario, there are simply three terms: a + b results in c. In Gurdjieff's Law of Three these are three independent *forces*': a + b+ X leads to c. The 'X factor' can be simply another element that enters into the situation, by chance or accident, to bridge the gap. Or that gap can be bridged by a *quality of conscious attention* – which is of course exactly the transformative teaching that will fall out of this body of work.

Let me you give you an example of how this oft-overlooked third force actually plays out. In school I was always taught that a sailboat moves through the water through the opposing forces of the wind on its sails and the water on its keel. When I actually learned to sail, I learned that this was not quite so. A boat locked in a tug-of-war between sail and keel does not move through the water; it rounds up into the wind and comes to a halt. In order to move in a direction, a third term must be added: the helmsman, hand on tiller, who brings the opposing forces into creative engagement so that a 'course over ground' can be established. The helmsman brings third force, and if you think this is simply too obvious to mention, try sailing a boat without one! It is often by missing the obvious that we remain locked in the impasse.

While the term 'Law of Three' is still pretty much limited to Gurdjieffian circles, the principle itself keeps getting rediscovered across a wide spectrum of intellectual disciplines. In an influential 2012 book *Design in Nature*, Adrian Bejan, a professor of engineering at Duke University, introduced what he touted as 'The Constructal Law':

> For a finite-size flow system to persist in time (to live), it must evolve in such a way that it provides greater and greater access to the imposed currents that flow through it.[7]

[7] Adrian Bejan, *Design in Nature* (New York, Random House, 2012), p. 3.

A 'flow system', Bejan explains, is anything with a current moving through it. It can be a river delta, the capillaries in a lung, the root system of a tree, or even a bustling air terminal or the worldwide web. His Constructal Law is in fact a textbook example of the Law of Three, in which affirming force is the current, denying force is the medium through which it flows, and reconciling force is provided by the algorithm 'Maximize access'. This is the reason that a tree root system, a human lung, and the Mississippi River delta all have such strikingly similar configurations; they are all designed according to the same template. Bejan calls it the Constructal Law. Gurdjieff calls it 'The Law of World Creation'. I rest my case.

The more important point to be made here is that since this law seems to keep getting itself rediscovered across the sciences and social sciences, there is a good body of confirming data now out there to suggest that it is, in fact, a universal template governing the arising of new phenomena, not simply the mad raving of a religious crank. Bejan himself has drawn on it heavily in his engineering work, and over the decades the principle has been tried out by Work people and others in a variety of situations ranging from marriage counselling to political action to successfully shedding ten pounds. I myself have worked with it as the still-unrecognized but powerfully intuited template that unlocks Boehme's complex cosmology. If threeness is, indeed, intrinsically connected to new arising, Christianity may be sitting on a larger theological market share than it has yet fully realized.

Gurdjieff himself hinted strongly that this Law of World Creation might have something to do with the Trinity. In his sprawling masterpiece *Beelzebub's Tales to His Grandson*, he explicitly equates the 'three holy forces of the sacred Triamazikamno' (as he calls the law here) with the three persons of the trinity:

The first, 'God the Father'
The second, 'God the Son' and

The third, 'God the Holy Ghost' – [8]

and while he claims primacy for the Law itself, it seems it seems fair to infer that he sees stewardship of this cosmic law as in some way uniquely entrusted to Christianity. Behind the presenting facade of the 'three God persons in community' – and working intentionally through them – stands the primordial divine constructal law giving rise to everything that is. Imagine *that* possibility as you revisit Bruteau's words: 'It is the presence of the Trinity as a pattern repeated at every scale of the cosmic order that makes the universe the manifestation of God and itself sacred and holy.'

Upon this cosmogonic foundation, of course, the three God persons in community rise beautifully. They are the first fruits of that divine will to manifest, and they make clear that what intends to be manifested in this

[8]   G.I. Gurdjieff, *Beelzebub's Tales to His Grandson* (New York and London: Viking Arkana, 1992), p. 688.

space is love. They are the guardians of the relational field —Teilhard calls it 'the sphere of the person' — in which all things will be brought to perfection in their own unique suchness. They remind us constantly that the purpose of this entire divine journey into form is to make manifest the fullness of love, the innermost secret of the divine heart.

Skillful means ...

More significantly, however, this link between the Trinity and the Law of Three puts into Christian hands a powerful, dedicated tool for both personal transformation and practical application in the world. Why is third force so easy to miss? Why do we so easily default back to a Hegelian dialectic? The answer, the Gurdjieff Work teaches, is that the human mind in its usual state is 'third force blind'. This is partly because of the skew of our rational mind toward dialectical thinking and partly because of the scrambled and distractable state of our attention. Without a different quality of conscious attention grounded in our body, we revert back to an 'either/or' kind of mental tunnel vision and miss the subtle cues that are coming to us both from our emotional intelligence and from the body's innate capacity to read the world through movement and gesture. Much of the practical training in the Work focuses on developing this more balanced 'three centered awareness'. When it is fully online, the real miracle occurs. We find ourselves increasingly able to partake directly of that 'luminous seeing' which was the original definition of contemplation ('knowledge impregnated by love') and bear it forth as skillful means into a world in continuous trinitarian transformation. The capacity to do this is what I mean by Wisdom.

Seen in this way, the Trinity indeed emerges as a tie-rod, the unifying thread through the whole Christian tapestry. It unites cosmogonic principle with empirical scientific reality, thus healing the split between religion and science. It reconciles cosmology and theology. It unites personal transformation and moral action in the world. And above all, it reopens those channels of devotion, symbolism, and sacrament, rejoining them linear rationality to create a single, spacious temple in which our Christian hearts can worship, transform, and grow.

I am speaking here not in theory, but out of direct experience – in fact, the most directly life-changing experience of my life. Gurdjieff holds a deep place in my life, but this is not simply on account of his teaching but because I feel that in a mysterious way his teaching was personally *transmitted* to me, as a sacred trust to which I would be held accountable. Little did I know when I arrived at Snowmass for that watershed Centering Prayer retreat that I was also about to meet the teacher who would put my worlds together. Brother Raphael Robin, the hermit monk and monastery handyman, showed up on the doorstep to deal with a frozen sink drain at the retreat quarters I had been assigned to. We soon discovered that we had Gurdjieff in common; Rafe had been had voraciously studying the Gurdjieff teaching on his own for more than twenty years. We each had a piece of the puzzle. I had the group training, the formal mentoring. He had the actual integration, the lived synthesis of his Christian mystical heart and the mindfulness he'd taught himself in trying to put the teaching into practical application. A year later I moved to Colorado to work with him full-time, and in the remaining two years of his human life we put the puzzle pieces together. In the alchemical fire of our work, the core elements of my theology were finally fused.

4

The Corner of
Fourth and Nondual

IT's A PUN, of course, shamelessly lifted from Thomas Merton's celebrated essay, 'A Member of the Human Race', in which he recounts the mystical lightning bolt that knocked him off his high horse and set the remaining ten years of his life on a whole new course:

> In Louisville, at the Corner of Fourth and Walnut, in the center of the shopping district, I was suddenly overwhelmed with the realization that I loved all these people, that they were mine and I theirs, that we could not be alien to one another even though we were total strangers. It was like waking from a dream of separateness, of spurious self-isolation in a special world, the world of renunciation and supposed holiness ... The sense of liberation from an illusory

63

difference was such a joy and a relief to me that I almost laughed out loud. And I suppose my happiness could have taken form in the words: 'Thank God, thank God that I *am* like other men ...'[9]

That revelation, exquisite in its particularity, leads to the conclusion, nearly everybody's favorite Merton lines:

At the center of our being is a point of nothingness which is untouched by sin and illusion, a point of pure truth, a point or spark which belongs entirely to God ... It is like a pure diamond blazing with the invisible light of heaven. It is in everybody, and if we could see it, we would see these billions of points of light coming together in the face and blaze of a sun that would make all the darkness and cruelty of life vanish completely ... I have no program for

[9] Thomas P. McDowell, ed., *A Thomas Merton Reader* (New York: Doubleday/Image Books, 1974), p. 345.

this seeing. It is only given. But the gate of heaven is everywhere.'[10]

What we see here is Merton in the midst of a revelation that is both unboundaried in its vastness and yet excruciatingly particular. It is *here;* it is at the corner of Fourth and Walnut; there are millions and billions of points coming together, but 'severally' – as Shakespeare would say, each in its own tiny pixel of blaze, in what Teilhard de Chardin would describe as 'a paroxysm of harmonized complexity'.

This is nondual, Western style: the corner of Fourth and Nondual.

The term 'nonduality' is a relatively recent acquisition in the spiritual vocabulary of the West. Merton himself never used it. It's what linguists call a 'loan word': a term imported through contact with another language or culture, in this case, the Asian spiritual traditions, which became wildly popular in the West during the second half of the twentieth

[10] Ibid., pp. 346-7.

65

century. The term caught on big time, essentially displacing the former Western 'unitive' to describe the highest states of spiritual realization, but there is still no consensus as to what the term actually means. Options range from a garden variety paradox-tolerance to a complete overhaul of the operating system of perception enabling one to see consistently from oneness – i.e., without intervention of the subject/object dichotomy. I myself prefer this more hard-edged end of the spectrum. Nondual is about *how* you see; what metaphysical bucket you put that seeing in is up to you.

Given my own longstanding interest in both meditation and the phenomenology of consciousness, it was pretty much a foregone conclusion that I would cross paths significantly with the metaphysical frameworks of the East, if for no other reason than that it is within these frameworks that much of the best work is currently being done. Many of the foundational roadmaps in the interspiritual and wisdom circles I mostly travel in have been developed by Ken Wilber, an ardent Buddhist, while the prominent names in the research field include other committed Buddhist practitioners such as Dan Segal, Matthieu Ricard, Evan Thompson, and Jon Kabat-Zinn. The conversation unfolds against a presumed Buddhist backdrop, and admission to this conversation table generally comes with implicit buy-in to the Four Noble Truths: that all life is suffering, that suffering is based on ignorance, that the transcendence of suffering is the goal of a realized life, and that the way to this realization is through committed spiritual practice. There is sometimes a further subtext as well: that attachment to a personal God is simply another form of ignorance, indicative of a still relatively immature level of conscious attainment. The nondual realms of consciousness are overwhelmingly presumed to be impersonal, and to the extent that Christianity is perceived to be 'stuck in the personal' it is often dismissed as lacking an authentic tradition of nondual attainment.

These assumptions were rampant – in fact, axiomatic – on the Colorado Western slopes where I cut my teeth on Centering Prayer during the early 1990s. They flourished in the lively interspiritual climate generated by Thomas Keating, himself a profound seeker along the pathways of nondual attainment. I am grateful to my monastic mentor Bruno Barnhart, longtime Prior of the New Camaldoli Monastery in California, for holding the line with his stubborn insistence that the Christian nondual path had its own intrinsic *gestalt*. 'The wisdom of Christianity does not find itself quite at home among the other sapiential traditions of the world', he wrote in his final book, *The Future of Wisdom*, following this observation with the even bolder assertion that our modern Western world in all its sprawling untidiness is not a deviation from the path of Christ but its legitimate and in fact inevitable trajectory. 'The apparent eclipse of Christian Wisdom by history is an optical illusion,' he writes, 'since history is itself the unfolding of the event of Christ.'[11]

[11]   Bruno Barnhart, *The Future of Wisdom: Toward a Rebirth of Sapiential Theology* (New York: Conntinuum, 2008), p. 186.

Like his role model Teilhard de Chardin, Bruno Barnhart was both a scientist and a mystic. He was fluent in the language of Eastern nonduality and counted Fr Bede Griffiths, Raimon Panikkar, and Beatrice Bruteau among his personal friends. But he was also fiercely grounded in a deep devotion to Christ and – again like Teilhard – was fully convinced that Jesus was not just a personal savior, but a cosmogonic master whose incarnation, death, and resurrection had literally shifted the foundations of the world. Because of its powerful Christic epicenter, the Christian experience of the unitive has a fundamentally different character from even its closest nondual analogues. Its energetic center is distinctly its own.

In other words, he would say, not all nondual attainment is alike. It is shaped by the metaphysical and cultural vessel in which it is received, and attempts to merge the streams too quickly simply result in muddied waters. A much more nuanced and respectful listening will be necessary before the terms can be accurately synchronized and the extraordinary tools coming to us from the east can be used to more fully excavate Christianity's own hidden treasure.

Where does this leave me? As usual, walking the razor's edge. Over the years I have been greatly assisted by the help coming to me from the Asian traditions. I have appreciated an approach based on phenomenology more than philosophy, that honors transrational knowledge rather than demonizing it, dialogues readily with contemporary science, and offers a direct bridge to spiritual practice.

Yet I remain firmly planted in a Christian theological ground: in the cosmic centrality of Christ, the reality of history, the goodness and importance of this earth, the alchemical necessity of suffering, the triumph of the cross. It is in my own Christian streambed that I have sought and found all of the cosmogonic pieces that have framed my theology. And in the end, when all the adjustments been made, when the terms 'nondual' and 'unitive' have been fully calibrated and levels of consciousness have been teased apart from *metaphysical assumptions* about levels of consciousness, I agree with my mentor Bruno that we will still see two qualitatively different expressions of the same nondual animal. Even at the highest levels of spiritual attainment, I believe that Christian nonduality will still hold fast to three core affirmations:

- the redemptive reality of suffering

- the endurance of the personal

- the 'scandal' of particularity

The emphasis will shift, of course, in a wider, and more unitive context. **Suffering** is less and less about substitutionary atonement and more and more about conscious love. The paschal mystery remains the epicenter, but it is now attached to an even more foundational cosmogonic mystery, the ultimate cost of the arising of anything at all. Suffering cannot be eliminated from the cosmic equation because, according to the Law of Three (to which, as I have argued, the Christian cosmovision is seminally linked), it is a necessary precondition of any new arising. Boehme links it with all three lines of action, but most frequently – and certainly in that first primordial arising of 'somethingness out of nothing' – it plays the crucial role of third force. Suffering cannot be dissolved, but it can be embraced and transformed, and for the Christian this is the alchemical pathway along which all unitive attainment will ultimately proceed.

The **personal** is no longer confined to the anthropomorphized versions of itself. God is no longer an old man with a beard, and personal prayer does not mean simply plowing through a punchlist of individual petitions. But the personal itself remains. Both Teilhard and Merton draw an identical distinction between an individual and a person. An individual lives for himself alone; a person knows himself or herself as belonging to a greater relational whole. An individual is what Merton was before his epiphany at the corner of Fourth and Walnut; a person is what he became in the wake of it. Teilhard, the paleontologist, takes this insight still a step further. Because of this cognizance of a greater relational whole, personhood reflects a greater degree of *symbiotic unity* and hence occupies a higher rung on the evolutionary ladder. The personal is for Teilhard the measure of relationality, and relationality is in turn the measure of *manifest consciousness within a system*.[4] Therefore, he argues, the highest levels of consciousness must necessarily be *more* personal, not less so, for 'higher' by definition means 'more relational,' and 'more relational' by definition means more personal. This same wisdom – that the highest manifestation of the divine nature unfolds within a relational (i.e., personal) field – is the mystery at the heart of the Trinity, which now re-emerges as the quintessential mandala of the Christian nondual.

To the extent that the Law of Three both assumes and requires **particularity**, the intuitive Christian (and in fact Western) predilection for the bits and pieces over the undifferentiated whole receives an even stronger cosmogonic validation. If Eastern versions of nonduality have traditionally tended toward the drop dissolving in the ocean, Western versions have traditionally tended more toward the ocean pouring itself fully into the drop. But even here the metaphor falls short, for it fails to take into account the wider relational field. Picture not just a single drop, but a vast ocean of drops, each one of them holographically containing the entire ocean. And now picture this ocean not as the Sargasso Sea but as the Gulf Stream, surging powerfully forward, destination unknown, propelled by its own mysterious inner current. That would be at least a beginning approximation of nonduality in Western mode.

In the end, it's a different taste more than anything else: simply the sense of a different kind of energy, flowing in a different direction. In one of his most brilliant short reflections Bruno comes as close as I've ever seen to evoking it directly:

> There is a secret in the heart of life that is not only the unmoving white light. It is not only the still point of the turning world, not only the light-filled empty center. It is also the lion of fire, the unceasing explosion of expansive being, of proliferating life, from the center. It is the fontal energy that demands to express itself everywhere and through every form ... it is not only the secret but the manifestation: the secret manifestation, the nameless, ubiquitous power that is expressed in our own restless centrifugal living.
>
> The gospel's secret power, often hardly glimpsed by Christianity itself, is the gathering up of all our passion, our entropic centrifugal energy, our very outward thrust and vital compulsivity,

secularity, and carnality, into this divine energy that ever flows out from its hidden Source.[12]

You can feel this same fontal energy surging though Merton's epiphany at the corner of Fourth and Walnut; it's what makes the experience so profoundly compelling. 'The gate of heaven is everywhere,' but it is also *somewhere*: 'in Louisville, at the corner of Fourth and Walnut, in the center of the shopping district'. And suddenly there is an electric current flowing between the immeasurably infinite and the infinitely particular. Both poles

---

[12] I am referring here to Teilhard's celebrated 'complex-ification/consciousness' theory, which states, essentially, that there is a direct correlation between the degree of complexity within a structure, and the degree of consciousness that structure is able to manifest. See Teilhard, *The Human Phenomenon*, p. 27. I myself quite prefer, however, Ilia Delio's marvelous Information Technology-inspired summary: 'Consciousness is, in a basic sense, the flow of information across complex levels of relationships; the greater the degrees of relationship, the greater the levels of information flow.' Ilia Delio, *Personal Transformation and a New Creation* (Maryknoll, NY: Orbis Books, 2016) p. 110.

are equally real, equally necessary to produce the current, which is how love makes itself manifest. Merton awakens from his dream of holiness into the reality of oneness, but even more, he awakens into the reality of *suchness.* In an outpouring of pure joy he directly sees and celebrates his kinship with each of these other myriad bits and pieces now finally recognized as equals, fellow pixels bound together in a common heart.

Some Merton aficionados will know that shortly before this epiphany, Merton had been working his way through Louis Massignon's French translation of a ninth-century Islamic treatise on the heart as an organ of spiritual perception, a mainstay of the Sufi mystical visionary tradition. That 'point or spark of absolute nothingness' Merton refers to in his final paragraph is originally the Arabic *srrr,* or 'secret,' the innermost veil of the heart. The teaching on seeing with the eye of the heart was obviously stirring inside him, and at the corner of Fourth and Walnut, that suddenly burst into a full bloom.

And so we are drawn once again to that mysterious convergence of 'heart', 'visionary seeing', and the direct infusion of a love of such clarity and generative force that it propels us back toward the world on wholly new and unpredictable paths of creative engagement.

For Merton, those paths would become the interspiritual dialogue, the peace movement, and civil rights. Ten years later he would die in Bangkok, under circumstances that still look suspiciously like a political assassination. In that tumultuous year of 1968 which also saw the assassinations of Martin Luther King and Robert Kennedy, the struggle between the old order and the new was rising to a fever pitch, and Merton's rapidly expanding cosmic heart was somehow caught up in the surge. Whether consciously or merely intuitively, his final self-offering was to be made in the midst of the very secularity and sprawling untidiness that Bruno[13] so unflinchingly named when he

[13] Bruno Barnhart, *Second Simplicity: The Inner Shape of Christianity* (Mahwah, NJ: Paulist Press, 1999), p. 21.

dared to proclaim that 'history is itself the unfolding of the event of Christ'.

Merton would no doubt be pleased to know that the corner of Fourth and Walnut no longer exists. It is now the corner of Fourth and Muhammad Ali Boulevard, renamed in 1978 in honor of one of this Southern City's most famous Black native sons. Truly, the gate of heaven is everywhere.

APPENDIX

'Where we come from ...'

On February 26, 2018, Cynthia offered this short lineage document to members of her Wisdom School network. It captures in a nutshell most of the essential elements in her unique synthesis of Christian Mystical and Fourth Way insights.

Wisdom, like water, is itself clear and formless, but it necessarily assumes the shape and coloration of the container in which it is captured.

Our own particular branch of the great underground river of Wisdom came to the surface about twenty years ago, flowing within two major riverbanks: a) the Christian mystical tradition of *theosis* – divinization – particularly as lived into being in the Benedictine monastic tradition, and b) the practical training in mindfulness and non-identification as set forth in the Gurdjieff Work.

The fusion of these two elements was the original accomplishment of my spiritual teacher Br Raphael Robin, who formed me in this path and sent me off to teach it just before his death in 1995. It is a distinct lineage within the wider phylum of *sophia perennis* – perennial Wisdom – and as with all particular containers, it has its own integrity and its own heart.

Here is my own quick shortlist of the seven main elements – or defining characteristics – for our particular branch of this Wisdom verticil:

1. We are founded on a daily practice of sitting meditation, predominantly but not exclusively Centering Prayer, anchored within the overall daily rhythm of 'ora et labora,' as set forth in the Rule of St Benedict.

2. We are rooted in the Christian mystical and visionary tradition, understanding contemplation in its original sense as

Cynthia with Thomas Keating

'luminous seeing', not merely a meditation practice or a lifestyle. In service to this luminous seeing, we affirm the primacy of the language of silence and its life-giving connection with the subtle realms, without which spiritual inquiry tends to become overly cognitive and contentious.

3. We incorporate a major emphasis (much more so than in more conventional contemplative circles) on mindfulness and conscious awakening, informed here particularly by the inner teachings of

G.I. Gurdjieff and by their parallels and antecedents in the great sacred traditions, particularly in Sufism.

4. We are an esoteric or 'Gnostic' school to the extent that these terms are understood to designate that stream of Christian transmission through which the radically consciousness-transforming teachings of Jesus have been most powerfully transmitted. But we steer clear of esotericism simply as mental or metaphysical speculation, and we affirm the primacy of the scripture and tradition as the cornerstones of Christian life.

5. Also in contrast to many branches of the Wisdom tradition based on Perennial or Traditionalist metaphysics (with its inherently binary and anti-modernist slant), we are emphatically a Teilhardian, Trinitarian lineage, embracing asymmetry (threeness), evolution, and incarnation in all their uncertainty and messiness.

Cynthia at the grave of Teilhard de Chardin

6. We are moving steadily in the direction of revisioning contemplation no longer in terms of monastic, otherworldly models prioritizing silence and repose, but rather, as a way of honing consciousness and compassion so as to be able to fully engage the world and become active participants in its transition to the higher collectivity, the next evolutionary unfolding.

7. Our most important teachers and teachings are Jesus, St Benedict, the canonical and Wisdom gospels; *The Cloud*

of Unknowing, the greater Christian mystical and visionary tradition (including Meister Eckhart, Jacob Boehme, Thomas Merton, Thomas Keating, Pierre Teilhard de Chardin, Ladislaus Boros, Bernadette Roberts), the Desert and Hesychastic traditions; Bede Griffiths and the Christian Advaitic traditions (including Raimon Panikkar, Beatrice Bruteau, and Bruno Barnhart); Rumi, Sufism, G.I. Gurdjieff. The poets: Gerard Manley Hopkins, T.S. Eliot, Dylan Thomas, Mary Oliver, Rainer Maria Rilke. And of course my own teacher, Br Raphael Robin.

My own teacher, Rafe